SURVIVING SIBERIA:
THE DIARY OF A POLISH GIRL, 1939–42

SURVIVING SIBERIA: THE DIARY OF A POLISH GIRL, 1939–42

Richard Spyrka

ARTHUR H. STOCKWELL LTD
Torrs Park   Ilfracombe   Devon
Established 1898
www.ahstockwell.co.uk

British Library Cataloguing-in-Publication Data.
A catalogue record for this book is available
from the British Library.

Arthur H. Stockwell Ltd bears no responsibility
for the accuracy of information recorded in this book.

ISBN 978-0-7223-4153-7
Printed in Great Britain by
Arthur H. Stockwell Ltd
Torrs Park   Ilfracombe
Devon

ACKNOWLEDGEMENTS

My mother, Jozefa Eva Rataj, is the rightful author of this book. She wrote it while she stayed in Valivade, a Polish settlement camp in the state of Kolhapur (now Maharashtra) near the city of Kolhapur, India. My mother wrote down her memories after her family journeyed through Siberia. I, her son, am only the translator.

My mother was born in March 1921. On 15 October 1945, at the age of twenty-four, she started writing her recollections of this journey and her experiences. When she passed away peacefully in July 2005, I inherited this diary. She often related her many recollections of her time in Siberia in a very vivid and detailed way. She was a wonderful storyteller. It was not until I read her written account that I started to realise what a profound effect it had had on her character and her attitudes to life. Throughout the translation, I tried to remain true to her storytelling spirit and to convey accurately to the reader what my mother was trying to say. I hope I have succeeded in this task.

I have dedicated this book to my two sons, Peter and Christopher, who were both very young when my mother passed away and were therefore unable to benefit first-hand from her experiences of life – they will have to receive that blessing from somewhere else. Hopefully, the translation and the passing-down of my mother's writing will go some way to redress the balance.

5

I would like to thank all my aunts and uncles, who patiently put up with my 'interrogations' in my quest to get as much background information as I could and to be true to the various unfamiliar words my mother used. I would like to thank Lucy, who stayed with us as part of our family and who at that time transcribed the original text to make it easier to read; and Tomek, my brother-in-law in Poland, who helped in the translation of the many unfamiliar Polish and Russian phrases my mother used; I would also like to thank my sister Maria for her good advice, her husband, Martin, for providing me with support at a difficult period in my life, and them both for their company and their hospitality.

And finally, to all who had a part in making the publication of this book possible – a big thank you!

A proportion of the proceeds of this book will be donated to the British Heart Foundation.

Valivade was a Polish transit camp in the state of Kolhapur (now Maharashtra), near the city of Kolhapur, in India. This is where my mother wrote her memoir. The camp was very well organised and became, within a very short space of time, a thriving town, complete with administration buildings, a regular newspaper, a church (which can be seen in the background), a hospital, an orphanage, eight community centres, a theatre, and a cooperative. The cooperative established a barber's shop and workshops for the manufacture of clothes, woven rugs, dolls and handicrafts. There was also a shoe repairer, a settlement canteen and restaurant, a postal service that regularly brought letters from Poland, and even a cinema house that showed Hindi movies. The Indian postmaster and his assistant learnt to speak Polish and many settlers spoke fluent Marathi. After the war ended, unable to return home to their native Poland, some settlers emigrated to Australia; some went to England.

15 OCTOBER 1945, VALIVADE, KOLHAPUR, INDIA.

On 1 September 1939 war broke out between Poland and Germany, war which would throw us far away across seas and rivers to Asia. Here we would wait and dream for the day when we would return to our humble homes, to the birds singing their magical songs in spring, and to the flowers that spread their precious aroma and fragrance and show their happiness in being in our garden. We long to return but it is still a dream! That we may one day return from our exile and hear the birds sing in our father's land that fed us and gave us life.

Yearning

O land of Poland! How I yearn for you!
When the clouds in the sky chase westward,
As they fade and disappear in the distance
My heart cries out, and my soul is sad,
And thoughts come to me in desperate mourning,
I dream of you and cry out for you.

O land of Poland! How I yearn for you!
Poor exile wandering for bread,
Discarded, like leaves in the autumn,
In distant, foreign, northern lands
I think, dream, all the time for you,
And wait for dawn, like the night waits for the sun.

8

O land of Poland! How I yearn for you!
Just like a plant on foreign soil
Losing its looks, freshness and scent
But continuing to live, dying in life,
Slowly withering with the passing of each day
With its crying and dying despair,
Like a lullaby – being rocked in the gentle breeze,
O land of Poland! How I yearn for you!

*My mother on the left, my mother's sister on the right
and a friend at the camp in Valivade.*

When war broke out I lived in a Polish settlement called
Bobiatyn in the district called Sokal which was in the province
of Lwow. Father had bought land there in the year of 1937 and
in June of that year I had left my family village in Bogucice

near Bochnia and, with my parents and younger siblings, settled in the land we had acquired. The beginnings were difficult as we had to build up our wealth and our newly acquired farm. By 1939, we were doing well and lacked nothing. Alas, this happiness did not last long. As soon as war broke out, everything that we had managed to scrape together in two-and-a-half years disappeared, as well as our happiness. The dark nights had started.

The Germans had already attacked Poland in August and on 1 September 1939, war was declared. I could not imagine what war was like and I was very frightened when I thought about whether the Polish nation would be able to oppose such a strong enemy. Nevertheless, after two weeks of open warfare, Poland fell and from the east the Russians crossed the borders of Poland and entered on to Polish lands. It would now be difficult to oppose two mighty powers. Now, and even before any Russians had crossed the borders, the Ukrainians started to show what they were capable of.

It was around 10 September 1939 and there were fugitives from the army everywhere. This was not surprising as the Polish authorities had given the order for all men who were of age, to move east and fight. We had our father's brother staying with us. One evening as we sat together, somewhere close to our settlement, fires started to appear on the horizon. We counted twenty-four fires which were blazing all around our settlement. Almost straight away we saw movement in our village. Anyone who had anything began taking it away from their homes and moving it somewhere into the fields: any cows which were in the cowshed, everything, as no one knew what would happen next. But thanks to the protection of God, our village was not touched. We stayed vigilant all night and no one went to sleep. I do not know what prevented them from attacking our village, whether it was all the commotion that had been created by everyone moving their belongings out into the fields, or whether it was the rumours that machine guns were hidden in the village. Maybe it was a combination of both. From this night onwards, every settler stood guard all night until morning, right until the time when the Russians arrived.

This is how they tormented us. First, the Ukrainians murdered many men and even women in the woods, stripping them of their money and clothes and then releasing them completely naked. Anyone who showed any opposition was dealt with in a most brutal way. The signs and clues were there for us and we were shown just how brutal they could be. As soon as the Russians arrived, everything changed and a new life began with a different form of murder.

The Poles were to be their friends. If you were a Pole, a Russian or Ukrainian you were all equal, you were all the same. Once they had calmed everything down they then started their own form of looting. Their first prey was the country houses, churches and the rich manor houses. As I went to church one day I saw a taxi going through the town and, in it, a beggarly-looking Russian who was badly neglected, wearing a dirty coat, all frayed and scruffy. I felt so much resentment towards him that I could not look at all the devastation he had caused. Furniture of all kinds lay by the church entrance and the rain poured on it. In this way, they tried to destroy all our good faith. They even managed to loot the graves of previous heirs. They threw out the body and they took the coffin with the sword. The town also started to become derelict and deserted. You could buy nothing and, when anything was available, the price started to rise to such a level that not one of us had sufficient money to pay for it. Our zloty stopped being used as currency and the rouble came into circulation. They started arresting priests and businessmen. Things just kept getting worse and worse, with the Germans tormenting us on one side and, on the other, Russians arresting people and taking them away to we knew not where.

In November 1939, the Soviets started digging trenches on our fields and as they required wood for the trenches, they would force people to do this work whether they liked it or not. Through their activity, they destroyed a lot of wheat which had been sown and caused a great deal of damage. This work continued until the end of December, when they stopped their digging as heavy snow had fallen. This was to be our first and last Christmas Eve under the occupation of the Soviets.

I can remember it, as if it were today, the eve of the birth of Jesus. I had always waited for this day with anticipation and a deep feeling of happiness as it was also my mother's name day. The Christmas tree and all the ceremony pleased me and made me happy. But on this particular Christmas, everything had changed and everyone felt depressed, sombre and in deep thought, thinking of the things that had now disappeared just like a soap bubble. When the day arrived we waited for the first star to appear. Mother had prepared all she could, but it was difficult to obtain anything as the Soviets had priority. Christmas Eve fell on a Sunday and therefore we were able to, on this occasion, start our feast when the first star appeared. We started together with our nearest neighbours. Father, as was the custom, took the unleavened bread in his hands and, after praying together, he began breaking the bread and sharing it with everyone in turn, giving them his Christmas wishes: for better Christmases and a free country. Later that evening we all got together and, as was the tradition, we went to our neighbour, Frank Rzemyk and his family. There we also shared and broke unleavened bread with one another, we started to sing carols and we all started feeling blissfully happy together.

We remembered the times past, which we had spent with all our families, without any worries as to what would happen tomorrow. I felt emotional at this time and, saddened – maybe because I knew, somewhere within me, that danger was hanging over us. At 11 p.m. we went to church, which was about five kilometres away in a little town called Tartakow. We walked to midnight Mass through the fields of Kopytowskie in the white snow, singing carols as we went.

The church was small, but richly adorned and was well known for its main altar, on which hung a picture of Our Lady of Immaculate Conception, and where many claims of miracles had occurred. During Mass the picture of Our Lady was revealed. After midnight Mass we returned to our homes and Christmas Day was celebrated as normal.

Our lives progressed very differently from the way they had before the war. Whatever thoughts and plans we previously had all fell apart. Young people no longer gathered as they had in the past, congregating in selected areas to talk and tell one another stories and tales to try to while away the time. Everyone was disillusioned, downhearted and depressed, wondering what would happen. With all this on our minds we had to look somewhere else for our entertainment, distraction, and things of this nature in an effort to utilise our youth.

During the day there was always something to do, but in the evenings I occupied my time reading books, like the trilogy written by Sienkiewicz, and they started to interest me more and more. There were three of us who read: my brother Janek, our neighbour Frank Rzemyk and me, and therefore our evenings passed like the blink of an eye and, before we knew it, Lent was approaching. On Ash Wednesday and the first Friday of Lent I went to the neighbouring church with Frank, on our sledges. This was to be the final day I would attend our church, which now seems so far away from us. God only knows if we will ever see it and our neighbours again; both remain etched clearly in our memories. On Saturday 10 February 1940, before the night sky had managed to clear and daylight descend, commotion and action started in our settlement – the likes of which I had never seen before. One Ukrainian and two Soviet personnel were sat on our neighbour's sledge. We did not know what the meaning of this was, but in a very short time we were to find out, and everything was made clear. At about 10 a.m. two sledges arrived for us which we were to travel on. I do not remember everyone who arrived to evict us out of our own house, but I remember one Ukrainian particularly. His name was Safron and he left a horrible impression on us. He read out to us, from a piece of paper, an order which sounded something like this: "The people here do not want you to stay any longer and therefore you must leave this place and transfer yourself to a different district, and in half an hour you must be ready." The order was read out in Russian by the Russian commander, but because we were unable to understand Russian, the Ukrainian made the translation.

Frightful scenes began to unfold as this Ukrainian came up to Father and started accusing him of hiding weapons. They started searching everywhere, under beds and anywhere where they felt something could be hidden, but fortunately nothing came to their attention and nothing was found. Mother was baking bread to feed us, but as they started to rush us and kept shouting, the bread was taken out of the oven practically unbaked and they would not allow us to stay any longer. The soldiers would not let us out of their sight and, whenever Father went out of the room to pack something, he would be followed by the Ukrainian pointing a rifle at him to prevent him running away. As a consequence, we took very little from our home because we were not allowed to and, secondly, there was not enough room on the sledges. We placed an eiderdown on the sledge and seated my younger brothers and sisters. On the second sledge, which was also not very large, we barely had room to take anything. Our family was, after all, quite large. There were nine of us: me, Mother, Father, Janek, Marysia, Tadek, Wladek, Zosia and, the youngest, Stasio, who was five years old. I do not know how to describe what I lived through at that precise time, when we were all departing from our family nest and about to go on our long wanderings. It was a horrible moment in time. Our dog, Alf, kept jumping up and down and started running after us as we were being pulled by the sledges, but when he received a strong kick, which the Ukrainian had aimed at him, he had to return. The dog was later taken in by our neighbours, the Rzemyks, who stayed in Poland.

We were taken to a neighbouring village called Bobiatyn and unloaded at the Russian school. There I met a lot of settlers, as well as many girlfriends who had already been sitting there for quite some time. At 2 p.m. they again told us to load up and we moved off to the station of Romasz. At 11 p.m. we arrived at the station and there they moved us into carriages which had, during the week, been prepared for us. These carriages had previously been used for the transportation of animals, namely cattle. Our carriage had one window and a plank bed, and in the middle there stood a heating stove. Squeezed into this carriage were sixty people; it was so tight it was impossible to move. After loading everyone, they closed the doors and pushed a metal latch to lock us in. It was only after two days that they took the latch off and opened the doors to check everyone's presence and then they replaced the latch as before. It was 13 February 1940 when we eventually moved off into the world and began our journey. We prayed, whatever prayers anyone knew at the time, and sang the hymn 'Under Your Protection'. We travelled only during the night, and during the day the train stood at small stations. On the third consecutive night, we arrived at the last station in Poland, called Sarny, and in the morning, on the Russian side of the border, they announced we would be transferred on to Russian carriages.

The Russian carriages were slightly bigger than ours but were in a worse condition – they had holes in them which made them draughty. We suffered as it was cold and, alongside this, hunger and starvation began. After a few days we started to receive soup, but it was soup which I had never seen or tasted before I had arrived in Russia. It was water which contained a few groats of barley and was completely without flavour. On several occasions we received bread, which again was completely tasteless and looked like a black, hard brick. Whenever we were let out to get water we were escorted by a guard who was armed, and he would not allow us to speak to anyone we met on the way. The people who lived in the areas we passed through looked very miserable and depressed. They wore long sheepskin coats, tough woollen shoes, big furry hats and gloves and in their hands they held wooden shovels, which they used for clearing the snow off the railway lines. We saw people of all ages working here. There were young boys and girls, but there were also elderly people working even though they could barely stand. At some of the larger stations we met other people like us from nearby villages like Chorochow, Nowogrodek, Baranowicze, etc. There were no toilets, so we had to use a hole in the carriage floor, or go outside and under the carriage when the train stood for longer. However, even when someone went outside for this purpose, an NKVD [Russian policeman] would be standing guard over them. I would guess it was around 28 February 1940 when we arrived in Siberia at the station of Seniegor and here we were unloaded.

Siberia

On the second day, there arrived a contingent of Russian sledge drivers and they started loading us on their sledges in preparation for the next part of the journey. Oh God, this mode of transport was absolutely horrendous. The cold frost was so severe you could hardly catch your breath and there was heavy snow everywhere. Mother sat on one sledge under the eiderdown and hugged the youngest children, Stasio and

Zosia, tightly to try to keep them warm. Father, Janek and I went on the second sledge and we too trembled and shook all over from the cold. At one village we stopped for a rest and to give the horses an opportunity to get their breath back. We learnt that three newly born children had died here. Although they had been carefully and warmly covered, it was to no avail.

After two days of travelling like this on the sledges we found ourselves in a town called Archangelsk where we were taken to a building which served as a transit camp. This building looked terrible. It had a large reception hall in which there were masses of people – so many that you could not move – the floor was dirty and on the walls you could see lice marching. This was the first abundant resource we had noticed in Russia in our first month. We somehow, through the grace of God, managed to endure the night, despite the fear that we might be overwhelmed by all this abundance of misery which surrounded us. In the morning, sledges arrived to take us to the place where we were to live. This last part of the journey took quite some time as we travelled through tundra – forests covered with terrible snow. On 5 March 1940 we arrived at our destination. Address: Ustianski region, Archangelsk area, Soleckaja base, in the village of Rzawki.

This settlement looked appalling. We were surrounded by forest. Within the forest, a clearing had been made in which stood a couple of barracks which we, the exiled, had to make our homes. There also stood two other huge buildings: one housed the canteen and stores, the other contained the bathrooms. Once we had settled in, they built two more: one was the school which my brother and sister attended and the other was the jail, which was where those who were under arrest for any offences were kept. We were told to unload our belongings and go to one of the barracks nearby. It was constructed with big wooden beams which were not planed but were rough, with gaps between the joints. Inside there were two large rooms, and in the centre an entrance hall.

Within the rooms the walls had not been painted – or even coated with anything – and two stoves stood on either side – stoves without tiles which I had never seen the like of before. Bunk beds, fashioned out of planks, filled the space around the edges, and in the middle of each room was a table measuring some five to six metres in length. Our room housed eighty-two people, which was overcrowded, and the smell was awful. My family and I lived in the upper plank beds, which we got into by climbing ladders – all of which had been made by the people who had lived here previously.

There were Ukrainians who had been living here from a place called Kiev. They had been sentenced to hard labour and sent here because they would not reject their faith. This was a serious offence and carried a heavy penalty. We received this information from one of them who had stayed behind after rejecting his faith and accepting the beliefs of the Russian form of communism – atheism. Because the room was open-plan, everyone lived there together – young and old – without exceptions.

In the morning, we were taken to the canteen where, with our money, we could buy soup – or rather water, barley groats and a kilogram of bread. We had hardly any money with us except five roubles, which Father had with him, and therefore we just managed to get through one day and for the next we had nothing left. On the second day, the commander, a man named Jergin, came in to chase everyone out to work . . . but what kind of work? After all, there were no fields here to which we were accustomed, just forest and more forest. My brother was suffering from frostbite in his feet and therefore could not get up, so the commander left him alone. Mother was lying down and was ill as she too had become frozen through on the journey; the rest were too young. Therefore my father and I had to go.

Father stayed by the barrack and helped with the construction of the new buildings and I went into the road with a shovel – the type which we had seen others using on the way here – and I cleared the snow away from the road to enable the tractors to bring in the wood. The work lasted eight hours each day. You had to arrive on time and you were not allowed to leave early – if the guards noticed you leaving early you were reported. After you were reported, you had to travel sixty kilometres to the town of Szangat and there the court would decide to reduce your earnings by twenty per cent. In this way, the fine was severe because reduced earnings meant you were unable to earn enough for bread.

In the evenings, when everyone returned from work, we would recite the Litany to Our Lady or to the Sacred Heart of Jesus. On one occasion we were saying our prayers together when in came Jergin who started making fun of us and mocking us for what we were doing, saying how stupid the young ones were for saying their prayers. He wrote down my mother's name and the names of the other women as it was forbidden to say any prayers to God. However, no matter how much they told us and tried to force us to stop, no matter how much they tried to get us to reject God, the more zealous we were with our prayers. It was only through prayer that we felt safe – it fortified us and gave us strength and courage; it helped each of us to carry our cross. We believed that, through prayer, God would not allow us to be lost and disappear for ever in a foreign country that did not believe in God – an atheist country – and that there would arrive a day when we would return to the land of our fathers, the motherland, Poland. We continued to pray because we felt that our prayers gave us additional courage, strength and bravery, and things just became that much easier. Our Lord Jesus was with us, all those who had been exiled, and he would take care of us.

On Sundays they did not allow us to celebrate, but chased us out of our barracks to work. However, when the Poles started to resist over and over again, they relented and temporarily allowed Sundays to be a day of rest. They started to realise that everyone worked better when they had time to do things for themselves, and also everyone needed rest. However, in the month of March we worked solidly without having any days off – this was their system and no one dared to challenge this. When Easter arrived they once again chased us out to work. Anyone who managed to escape into the woods was OK, but anyone who remained in the barracks just could not get out of doing work – the guards made sure of that. In the month of May, 'rafting' was always and traditionally carried out. It is difficult for me to describe what this was.

I had never seen nor heard of anything like 'rafting' in Poland and therefore everyone was curious to find out what this was. The guards kept saying in their broken Polish to us, 'There are lots of everything, lard and butter, as much as you like, but there is also a lot of work.' On 20 May 1940 the rafting started.

They gathered all of us, including those who genuinely could not work, out in the snow. The only ones who were left behind were the elderly and the very young children. They herded us to another settlement close to our own which was about eight kilometres away and which was home to Russian workers. We saw and met many of the Russian people that lived in the area and what a sad and depressing impression these people left on us. They were poor, their wretched feet were bandaged with cloth, over which they wore slippers made from birch bark, women wore dresses made up of many patches and the men wore ragged trousers. Their houses were very modest, and looked like they had previously been used as barracks as they were very similar to ours, with one difference: they were slightly smaller and were divided into rooms and in each room there lived a family. There were some who owned a cow, some who owned a goat, but there were also those who owned nothing.

We spent some time in the square and we managed to get a

good look around. After some time, we were given large wooden poles with a hook on the end which were to help us push timber away from the riverbank. At 11 a.m. they led us to the river which was called the Solica River. Nearby, there were large stacks of timber laid out and it was this timber that we had to throw into the river. We worked in 'brigades' and each chief brigadier had seven to ten people working for him. He controlled them. Earning for the brigade was dependent on how many stacks of timber were thrown into the river. After the first day's rafting the routine was as follows: at 4 a.m. there was a bell which was sounded, informing everyone to go for breakfast. At 5 a.m. everyone went to their place of work and they were there until 10 p.m. Lunch and evening meals were brought to us where we worked and breakfast and dinner were eaten in the canteen. A lot of the money we earned was spent on food while we were working as we did not always have the time to take what they brought for us to eat and sometimes it was inedible. Therefore when we received our pay for the rafting there was not enough money left for anything else. We earned either 50 roubles, 90 roubles or 110 roubles, which was the highest pay. This rafting went on for at least thirteen days and was very dangerous.

After the rafting had ended some of us received work at the base, but the vast majority of us returned to our settlement. Father, my younger sister and I stayed on and helped trim the wood before stacking it in the large holding area. When we finished the work I, with my younger sister, would go and pick cranberries for Mother to make jam for our one piece of bread. My younger brother, Janek, managed to get himself work as a hammer beater in the smithy, where he worked very hard, the smithy being about twenty-five kilometres away in a village called Szostowa. Despite all this hard work and the money we received, it was still not enough to keep all of us and the five who were not working. On countless occasions I would go to work hungry and without food and return home at the end of the day to find nothing to put into my mouth, and therefore I would go to bed and fall asleep with nothing to eat. I worked like this for one month to prepare the timber, and then they moved us on to carry out different work nearer the barracks.

In the morning, after we had eaten breakfast, we went into the woods where we would cut down trees and then sort them out into different thicknesses. The larger ones went together and the smaller ones separate.

I do not remember the precise date, but in July we received information that we had to prepare ourselves to be taken to carry out some rafting in another region. At this time, my legs were covered in sores and therefore I went to see the doctor. However, she did not agree that I was ill enough to be excused from work; in fact, she stated that by going my condition would improve and the healing process would speed up as it was dry there! Therefore, every morning in July, usually at 10 a.m., we (mainly the young settlers) set off to the base and were given two sledges which were to take our possessions which we were carrying, and then we continued with our journey. Commander Jergin went with us as no one else knew the way. We went over valleys, dales and through the fields, and we saw many poor villages. We were frightened even to look at the people who lived there as they looked so wretched.

The journey was long, about eighty kilometres, and therefore we had to stay overnight in one village and it was only in the morning that we moved off again. On the second day, we reached the River Usi, which we crossed on a raft. The river was quite wide and had a strong current. On the other side of the river stood an orthodox church without a cross. The church was closed, and boarded up completely. A few metres away there was a small cemetery and I noticed that there were still a few crosses on the graves.

After we crossed the river, our journey went a lot quicker.

Although we were tired, we learnt from the Soviets that when we reached our destination we would meet other Polish people from other settlements. There was still a long way to go, but we were overcome with emotion and happiness at the thought of meeting others who were in the same situation as we were and whom we might know. We almost ran the rest of the way. On the journey we kept meeting more and more people; we became livelier; we could hear the river at the side of the road, and the timber in the river creaking in the log jam. By evening, after running most of the way, we arrived at our destination, which was Rubiesz. There we met many Poles – there were a few familiar faces and I knew some of the girls.

We were allocated a workers' house, which was a house on stilts, sitting in the water. Inside, there were plank beds and some hay. Everyone, as best they could, settled themselves in for the night, but despite everything it was freezing and all night I was shaking from the cold. In the morning, we received our tools and got to work. Oh Lord! How difficult and dangerous this work was!!

The girls stood in the river, slightly higher than the logs and pushed the logs out. The boys would stand on the logs; a few of them who could barely stand on their legs would bend over in a variety of contortions, one way and then the other. They would push the logs further out using their wooden poles and with the hooks they would separate them so they could freely float down the river. They had to be agile and jump from one log to another. As this was going on another group would be throwing more logs from the pile on the riverbank into the river. We worked hard and the time flew by quickly – just like the river flowed – and the ten days of rafting were over – as fast as a bullet shot from a rifle. On the ninth day, one of the logs fell on my leg and hit me so hard that it took the skin off; I was very lucky that my leg was not broken. After that, I was unable to go to work, but was laid up in bed writhing in agony. On the eleventh day, it was time for us to return home and back to our village. There were two of us who were unable to walk and therefore they gave us sledges and we set off for Rzawki.

The rest of the group followed the river and at the same time kept a watchful eye on the logs in the river. Wherever the logs became trapped, forming a log jam, they would ease them away from the riverbank so that the logs could continue their journey down the river.

When I returned to Rzawki, I was laid up for a month after being given a discharge note excusing me from duty, for which you were paid a certain percentage of your previous ten weeks' earnings. When we were in Rubiesz we earned, which was an exception, good money, because here we were in a different region and we were not swindled or cheated. We were paid what we were due and the correct rate for the work we did.

Summer in Siberia lasted only for a short time, barely two months, and then immediately there came the fearsome cold winter. During this warm period there were huge amounts of berries we could pick: raspberries, cranberries and huge amounts of mushrooms. Mother would go with my youngest brother into the woods to pick mushrooms and blackberries. They would sell some of these and the rest they would bring home for us to eat to keep the hunger at bay. I remember, one day, after coming home from work (I was working by the roadside clearing stumps of wood at the time), I saw Mother and my brother sitting under the eiderdown and barely alive from tiredness and fright. Mother started telling us what had happened – they had got lost in the woods and, no matter how hard they tried, they could find no way out. God, how lucky they were to have got out of the forest before nightfall; there had been many cases of others who had got lost and had never returned.

I also remember a time in spring; it was a Sunday and my brother Janek was home from Szostowa, where he worked. As it was a Sunday, we wanted to make it special and we wanted Mother to prepare something special to eat; however, there was nothing. So, I set off with my sister and another girl to the woods to pick some mushrooms called *smerdze,* which people had said were poisonous, but they had eaten them and nothing had happened – no one had died and everything was all right. We hadn't picked very many, but as we were returning across the river on the footbridge, my foot slipped on the wood and I fell into the river. If I had been on my own that would have been the end of me, as the river was very fast-flowing, and there was a swell. I would have lost my life, sacrificed for a few mushrooms.

When we brought the mushrooms home to Mother she boiled them, added a few groats of barley she had bought and straight away we had a little more to eat. Starvation is a terrible thing. When you are starving you are unable to think about anything else except satisfying your own hunger, and I am sure this was the desire of everyone else.

It was easier for us to survive through the summer, but the winter was so difficult and a terrible strain. Firstly, there was the lack of proper covering for our feet, as well as inadequate clothing. Secondly, we had starvation staring us right in the face because, unlike in the spring, there was nothing we could gather or pick to supplement any meals we had. The snow had already fallen by September and there was other work to do. The men were allocated work loading timber on to the sledges; others did unauthorised work for cash; and the girls did work known in Polish as *trylowka.* I was involved in this abhorrent *trylowka.*

I was at the workers' house when Makorski, who was the guard in charge of the forty-sixth quarter, arrived and required seven girls for *trylowka.* I was not well at all and went to see the nurse to request a sickness certificate for a few days. However, it was not to be, and not even the nurse could help me as she was under strict orders not to issue any sickness certificates. Therefore I had no option, and at 2 p.m. we set off to the forty-sixth quarter. The journey was quite long; I do not remember exactly how far it was, but it was at least twelve kilometres because it was evening when we arrived at the place. They allocated us to one of the barracks and immediately set us to work the day after. Very, very early we went to the canteen for breakfast, and later they gave us a horse and a sledge on to which we had to load timber and take it to the storage facility. I worked for two excruciating weeks – two weeks of wading through snow up to my waist, frozen to the core of my bones. My body was beginning to fail me. I could barely endure this suffering. I became ill and, because there was no nurse, I went back to the base to see Dr Julia, who gave me a sickness certificate for a whole week. At the end of the week I was only just beginning to feel better and on that last day I was told I was to go back to work. The guards threatened that if I stayed sick without a certificate I would be officially on report and, if this happened, a percentage of what I earned would be deducted. I was given work in the second quarter and I had to clear snow from the timber which had been stocked. The work was not difficult, but the pay was less – not even enough to feed myself. The frost was severe, minus forty-five degrees, which caused us pain and was difficult to endure. There were times when it was even colder, but they would not allow us to stop working.

I remember it was the year 1941 in December, just before Christmas; the frost was so severe it was difficult to tolerate. At the same time, some of our men had frostbite on their hands and feet, but not even this helped us in our cause. I spent Christmas 1941 in one of the quarters, completely isolated from my family, among only friends and my girlfriends. There was no talk about any of us not going to work on such a huge holy day when we celebrated the birth of Christ in Bethlehem, when the Christmas tree had to be prepared. No one thought of not going to work without a doctor's certificate and no one was issued with one either as the authorities decided that, because this was a very important day for the Polish people and was traditionally spent at home with the family, anyone who applied for one was 'trying it on'. So, we went to work as usual and everyone went, even those who could not, and after work in the evening we set up and decorated our Christmas tree.

At the table, everyone allowed themselves a little more than normal and we broke normal bread, as opposed to the traditional unleavened bread, as we passed on our wishes to one another. All this happened in a strange and quiet mood, not the way it would normally happen among young people. After our humble feast, we all gathered in one of the barracks where the men lived, and there we dressed the Christmas tree, which they had brought from the woods. There was barely anything on it except a few scraps of white paper and a few candles, but it did remind us of our Polish Christmas trees. We sang Christmas carols and there were many there, both girls and boys, who shed a tear. Everyone tried to keep their emotions at bay so as not to further aggravate their nerves, not to fall on their spirits, as everyone believed that there would arrive a day of redemption, that this suffering must end and that we would be able to look everyone in the eye confidently and say, "You were unable to destroy us, to wrench our faith from our hearts and now it is time for you to answer the question: *Why?* No one stood up and made any declaration of intent, but everyone was convinced that it would change and we would return to our loved ones, where our family roots were.

We spent many days and nights like this: working, despite the hunger and cold, cut off from the world without newspapers or any other form of news. We sat in the forests and we knew nothing except about those things that directly affected us and surrounded us. This monotonous humdrum way of life quickly sickened all of us. Letters from our friends back home in Poland stopped arriving because war had broken out between the Soviets and Germans, and life became more and more intolerable. We could not get sufficient bread for all of us as this was rationed with ration books. Those not working could get 400 grams and working people got 600 grams. Each day soup was made out of water and even this was limited. It contained a few groats of oats and barley with a couple of bones thrown in. The second winter spent in Siberia was even worse and gave us serious signs of what was still to come. By summer it was worse still.

The clothes we possessed had become very tatty and were falling apart, but we had no other clothes, no replacements and nowhere to get any new ones. Often, illness would befall someone and we were then forced to bring out any reserves we might have in an effort to rescue them from starvation and try to conquer the nightmare that we might die in this godforsaken place.

In February, my brother Janek fell ill after injuring his leg at the smithy. Father and my two younger brothers, Tadek and Wladek, took him to the local hospital and my brother lay there for two months. My father too spent some time in hospital, but I cannot remember for how long. I thought that this would be the end of us as without the extra money from work completed by my father and brother there was nothing to take out of our stores; what could we take to sell to buy some bread? But our God and our Holy Mother kept us under their protection and somehow we managed to live through this crisis.

Summer came and, once again, we had to use our wits to stay alive. Our meals were supplemented with mushrooms and berries, and very often there was more of this food than there was bread. Our second season of rafting the timber came and went, after which they moved us a long, long distance away from our village of Szostowa. This village lay some twenty-five kilometres from our settlement. It looked poor and the landlords looked even poorer. They worked in the fields and were unable to make ends meet. They owned a small piece of land in which they planted their potatoes. I met many who, in their homes, kept a picture of Our Lady hanging discreetly out of sight. When I asked them why they tried to hide the picture, they would tell me tearfully that they have to hide it away from their own children because if the children knew that their parents had a picture and prayed, they would tell the authorities and the parents would be arrested. I was given the same explanation on many occasions.

All the girls were allocated to one room, just girls, and there were two barracks allocated for the men, who were of all ages. Next, we were assigned work. Some of the other girls had to load wood on to the sledges, and what I was told to do was not really hard work, but we had to walk everywhere in the woods, where there were many paths and marshes. We would walk with a scythe and a rake and we would either be cutting the grass or gathering the grain using the rake.

We took our food with us to work every day. This consisted of dry groats of barley, some flour, oil and 600 grams of bread. On many occasions, this work in the woods could last three or four weeks at a time and was spent away from the settlement. Fortunately, the time went very quickly and spending it together could be quite pleasant. While we were working we sang a variety of songs and on the road home to our house, which was in the wood and had a very small door through which even I had to bend down to get through, we picked a whole variety of mushrooms: *kozaki, leszki, borowiki, rydze* and many, many others, which I did not recognise. We prepared these mushrooms for our dinner and used them sparingly so we would be able to share some with our families and with those who did not work – they could not live off only 400 grams of bread.

When we returned from cutting the grass we were sunburnt, dirty and tired. In this dog's kennel – this is what we called our home in the woods – lice did not give us the opportunity to sleep. There was no shortage of these tiny creatures; they were everywhere, even in houses where no one lived at all, and we even came across some in the fir trees. It was in Russia that I first encountered mites, and they left their visiting card all over my body in the form of sores. Furthermore, my shirt was always covered in small red marks from the blood of the many lice which I had killed. Lice, nits and mites were the greatest wealth that Russia possessed and we were introduced to them on our arrival.

After I finished doing this work I was moved to help load the timber and I was attached to one of the brigades. Our brigade consisted of five people: three men and two women. The work was hard and the journey was particularly tiring as we had to trek eight kilometres and because of this we had to set off very early every morning. I worked in this brigade for quite a long time, almost to the start of winter. Time went quickly. Day after day came and went, and our future remained unclear. We existed and lived one day at a time.

On one occasion when I went to work (just like any other day) quite early in the morning, I had an accident. I hit my arm with an axe. I was cutting branches down from trees when my hand slipped and I struck the other arm. Luckily I was wearing a long glove, but I still sustained a gaping wound and I now have a scar which acts as a reminder of this incident to this day. I immediately closed the wound with my other hand to try to stem the flow of blood, ran to the river and placed it in the water to keep it clean once again and to try to stop the blood flow. Immediately the guard instructed me to leave. I went to see the nurse so she could put a bandage on the wound.

For over a month I did not go to work and my arm hurt badly, but we still had to eat, so I used to steal away with all the younger children into the woods to pick blackberries. In the evenings, I would sell the blackberries which I had picked and, in this way, I at least earned some money and was able to feed myself. In fact, picking and selling the berries proved to be a more lucrative task then doing the best-paid work that was available. Soon, however, my arm healed up and the officer in charge of our area, who looked reasonably pleasant, showed me the road where I was to work.

It was the beginning of September 1941, and what work it was! There were possibly a couple of men, I do not at this moment remember how many, and ten girls, and we would walk deep into the forests, through marshes, bogs and thickets, until we arrived at the place where we would start to clear the wood. We would coppice any tall trees and remove the stumps of previously felled trees from the ground. Our lunch was very innovative; when we were setting off, we received bread from the canteen, including another 400 grams for lunch in the woods, and with this some soup. During this time the main 'soup of the day' contained meat and one portion cost 1 rouble and 50 kopeks. If you couldn't afford this, there was also fish soup, which cost 75 kopeks and which tasted bland and was entirely liquid. Even to this day, when I recall how this fish soup tasted, I almost retch; that's how good it was – so *good* you could not even eat it. There were times when I took nothing to the woods except this runny soup and some bread and that is all I had for two days. I had meat soup on only one day as it was too expensive for me to buy; therefore for lunch in the forest all we had was the bread that was left over from breakfast. I recall these events with great difficulty as I seldom had bread for lunch. I was so hungry on the journey that I would eat it. Therefore, for lunch, we would go to the woods and search for mushrooms, which we would put on the end of a stick and roast on the fire. When we were returning home, every one of us tried to keep some mushrooms with us so that we could have some for dinner, as there was never enough food in the canteen. When I got home in the evening, the mushrooms were immediately sorted and my brother and father helped me to clean them up and boil them in a pan. The meal was so tasty, so appetising, even without any seasoning added – just water, salt and occasionally some onion, which was very difficult to obtain. Sometimes, for dinner, they would prepare for us powdered millet with cooking oil and I would mix two portions of this in the mushrooms and again the taste was enhanced. This is how God never forgot us; although it was difficult even to earn enough money to have this piece of black bread, which was limited and on ration books, we supplemented it with mushrooms and berries. But, as winter drew closer, it again became more difficult to find mushrooms, and as a consequence life became worse for us.

GOOD NEWS

It was around 25 November 1941; we had returned from working and it was bitterly cold outside. We all huddled around the fire, trying to warm ourselves up and dry our socks, when the guard came in and gave an order for us to report to the officer in charge. We were all frightened and bewildered; what could this be? But an order is an order and we went. In the office the NKVD officer was sitting and waiting for us and was even smiling. He ordered us to sit down and, as if from a prepared script, started to ask questions: When and where were we born? What districts, village, etc? And he noted everything down very carefully. At the end he stated that we were free to leave, that we could choose whatever work we wanted to do and no one would stop us. He talked to us in a different way, a different tone and was more civil than he had been previously. Such happiness overwhelmed us and it is difficult to put this into words.

We were overjoyed; no one slept during the night; everyone prepared themselves and their things for the future. Our spirits were uplifted with the thought that we would now leave these Siberian forests and return to our family lands. In the morning, when I woke, I was tired but happy and uplifted in spirit. I went to work with different thoughts; different ideas were coming into my head and different possibilities presented themselves before my eyes. Work was still necessary as we had to go in order to receive a piece of bread;

if we did not go we received no bread. The guards no longer had the right to chase us out to work as they had before, but if anyone did not go they received no bread or soup. Winter arrived and I found myself for the third time working at the settlement in the forest.

This last winter left marks on me which would have serious consequences. The snow fell so heavily that it was waist deep and, if by chance you fell over, it was very difficult to get up. It was so cold and freezing you could hardly catch your breath. Father, brother and my sister all worked at the base, but despite this there was still not enough money coming in to feed us all. Whatever Mother had, she would give me to sell, and there was nothing that could help us except our belief that we would leave – this was the only thing that kept our spirits up. People were suffering badly through the Siberian winter, and more and more we began to see people leaving.

In November, many started their travels to the nearest town, which was around sixty-four kilometres away. More and more news kept arriving as some of those who left returned to tell us that the people in neighbouring settlements were travelling to a place beyond the river. At last, we got to know exactly what was going on when a commander from the NKVD confirmed that preparations were being made for an exodus to warmer climes and that the Polish Army was being formed in the East.

In our settlement there was lots of activity as everyone hurried to prepare themselves to get away as quickly as possible. People walked, young and old, sixty-four kilometres through the thick forest, taking no notice of the difficulties or any of the accidents that might happen on the way. One time a man, who seemed in good health and strong, had come to check everyone's papers, but on his return through the forest road he had stopped and sat down, and it turned out that when he sat down it would be for ever – he never got up. We knew this because the Soviets, who drove past, found him covered in snow, stiff. However, no one would be put off, not even in these freezing conditions, and masses of people set off on their journey. Oh my God! What a journey it seemed, so bad was the Siberian freeze, and there was such great snow! A terrible nightmarish scene, and anguish for the Polish nation!

Everyone took all the belongings they had – their last eiderdowns, anything to sell in order to have some money on them. They would make sledges themselves and stack on their few belongings and the other things they had bought and pull this all the way to the town, sixty-four kilometres from our village. Many succumbed to frostbite on their hands and feet and many fell so ill that they remained behind at the nearest kolkhoz in order that they might regain some of their strength. Those who reached the town were either given a horse and cart or were put on a train to carry on their journey, but where they were going they did not know, and for what they did not know.

We, for the moment, were not thinking of leaving as we had nothing and we did not even have anything to protect ourselves against the severe frost. Father and Janek continued to work at the base, both of them at the forge as the blacksmith had left. I worked in the woods and in different brigades as people kept leaving our settlement and there were fewer and fewer people left to work. As soon as people had just enough, they would leave. Eventually, there were only a few families left and I had no one to go to work with. So I did not go to work. It became harder and harder, and when I think about these times I despair. Others were able to leave as they had saved resources; we had nothing, not even enough clothes to keep us warm. When I remember these times it moves me to tears.

Father managed to arrange for us all to move to the base, so we were once again all together. The person in charge at the base gave us a separate room which was very small, but it had to suffice. We had a stove just like in Poland, on which to cook, and a plank bed by the wall on which we slept, side by side like sardines. Christmas was drawing closer, but we still did not have enough to enable us to leave and, more and more, there were continuing signs of starvation. One day, my brother Janek was working in the smithy and he burnt his leg. As a consequence, he was laid up for two weeks. I had to substitute for him at work, and therefore I would go with my father; if I had to use the hammer I would, and I would do anything else that required doing. We received no pay at all except an advance of 20 roubles, and starvation continued to be a threat. Father's legs swelled up and he was unable to put on his wool boots, but someone had to work as we had to eat. We therefore devised all sorts of different ways to overcome this hardship and somehow fight it off to the end.

In our village there were quite a lot of horses and many which looked half starved and ready to die, which of course many did. When any died, and before anyone could get rid of the body, our people would gather around it and try to obtain at least one piece of horsemeat. Tadek went a number of times and managed to bring something back, but later even this was very hard to come by. We started to hunt for dogs.

This too was a difficult task as there was nowhere to prepare the dog. There was one time in the evening when we had absolutely nothing to take away our hunger. Father and Janek decided that they must somehow catch and kill a dog. That evening they enticed a dog to our room and somehow managed to kill it. I do not know how as I ran away; I was frightened that the Soviets might suddenly appear and cause trouble. Thank God, luck was on our side, and although the dog whined and barked, it did not attract anyone's attention. The next day we had a tasty dinner. Mother melted a litre of fat out of the animal, and the meat was so tasty. In Poland, pork is thought to be the tastiest of meats, but I did not know that dog meat could be so tasty. How could we have known? Dog meat was never eaten in Poland and no one would even dream of this possibility. This meat did not last long and was eaten quickly. It was difficult to hunt down more, but somehow we managed to kill another dog; this time mother prepared the meat for our journey. The fat was once again melted out of the carcass, the meat roasted and placed into the pan containing the fat. This cooled down beautifully and looked just like jellied meat. We had started in earnest to prepare ourselves for the long road ahead.

My brother still had a suit and a pillow which was not needed for the road. These I took to sell in order that we might have some money. I sold the suit for 250 roubles and for the pillow I received 90 roubles, so we already had something. At the base they were selling woollen boots as well as padded trousers. On Saturday Father bought a pair and on Monday he did not go to work; instead he went to the village in order to sell something. Nikicim, who was one of the officials, arrived soon after and he went straight for Father, asking him why he had not reported for work. Did he not know that if he did not work he would receive no food? Father was not all that frightened or surprised and started to say that surely they must know that everyone is leaving and that we were also going, and, after all, Janek had informed the officials, had requested his pay and had handed in his notice, along with my father's.

No amount of explanation would help. When I went for bread, they took away my ration book and it was only with great difficulty that I managed to obtain some soup. After we had had breakfast, my brother went to receive his pay for working, and the official asked us to bring all the things we had bought and to come to the stores where he would pay us. After we gave him our statement the official in charge of the base stated that he would never pay us off, because Father had 'conned' him and had taken the woollen boots, but not gone to work. Tough, but what could we do? We decided to leave without pay if only they would give us some bread. They would not even agree to this and insisted in an unbelievable way that Father must return the boots; if he did not, we would receive no bread.

There ensued a nightmarish incident, which occurred when the official came into our room just as father was putting on his boots. Father was holding them and then the official was holding them, arguing that Father should return them, and if he did not he would not be allowed to leave and no bread would be given to us for our journey. It was an awful day, the arguing, the disagreement, but none of us lost our nerve and we agreed that on the following day we would go to the town to see the commander of the NKVD.

My brother and I set off, very early in the morning without telling any of the officials. Our journey was terrible as the wind was howling and the air was freezing, as was normal for this time in Siberia. Despite warm clothing, my legs felt as if they had been cut with a knife, and blood was oozing out of them. We hurried in order to reach our destination by the end of the day, which would not be easy as we had a long way to travel and the roads through the forest were covered with snow. It was 10 p.m. in the evening when we reached the town.

I had already been here before and therefore I knew which houses Poles had occupied, but they had all gone. A Russian lady who lived in one of these houses was quite friendly, but was unable to tell us anything. To some extent, she was complaining and stating that everyone had left about two weeks ago, and that is all she would tell us. We therefore set off to find somewhere to stay as it was already late.

We arrived at one house, but the owner was not in, only her children. I could understand them and we talked, and I felt that we would be allowed to stay. We therefore went over to the canteen and sat down at the table for something to eat. There we could get some soup and 100 grams of bread. We ate this 'like a dog eating a fly', for what was this for someone who was so hungry? We ate and then went to see the landlady, who had by this time returned. She greeted us politely and confirmed that she would be able to give us a bed for the night where we could sleep and rest. She talked to us pleasantly and even discussed with us her own misfortune: her husband had been taken away and she had been left to suffer with the children. For sleeping, she prepared us a plank bed on which we placed a mattress, but the covers were poor and it was cold. Both my brother and I laid ourselves down to sleep. It was quite uncomfortable, but I was grateful that we had found somewhere to sleep.

In the morning when it was still dark, our landlady got up and boiled some water and potatoes. She invited us to join her and gave us what she could. By this time it had become light so we thanked our landlady for letting us stay overnight and we set off on our way to the commander of the NKVD. When we eventually arrived, he welcomed us and dealt with us in a very civil manner. He stated that if we had proof of our purchases then they had no right to hold us back, and if Father had bought the boots for cash then they had to give us bread for our journey. He told us to return to our settlement and to set off on the road, and in the meantime he would telephone ahead and talk to the officials about this matter. We were pleased at the results of our meeting and we made our way to the stores where bread was being sold. This was the first time that we went to obtain bread and we managed to get more. My brother had scratched off our quota somehow and changed it so we managed to get enough bread for ten days – 36 kilograms. As we were not prepared for this, we had no sack to place the bread in, in order to carry it the long distance. With nothing to carry it in, this would be an impossible task. I therefore went to a lady's house and here I took off my head scarf and skirt (which for warmth I was wearing on top of my dress). I managed to tie these together and place the bread inside. This was how we managed to carry the bread back to our settlement.

I will never forget this journey as I suffered and it took its toll on me. We left the town at about 10 a.m. – I suffered more from the cold than the weight I was carrying on my back. We reached the village, where we were to stay overnight, very late in the evening; everyone else was asleep except our landlady, and it was as if she knew that we would be returning late. Straight away she let us into our room and prepared our bed by the stove. There we gave a huge sigh of relief as we were out of the terrible cold and the freezing conditions.

In the morning, we set off again, as we still had a long way to go. It was very difficult to walk and keep our eyes open as the fleas had been biting us all night and we had been unable to get any sleep. Even in our settlement we too had fleas, but they seemed to be much more considerate, at least allowing us to sleep peacefully at night. We reached our settlement very late in the evening, but we had our precious bread, and again we gave a huge sigh of relief as we now knew we had at least some bread for our journey. When we got back we did not return to the building we had left as the main official at the base had turned our family out and put us in a larger room on the outskirts of the base. Almost straight away another official arrived and told my brother to come to the office, where he would be given bread for the journey. As it was late, we decided we would collect the bread in the morning and that we would try to leave the day after. However, it did not work out this way because the sledge we had arranged to take us was commandeered by one of the guards, who tried to prevent us from leaving. It was not until the day after that I managed to arrange another sledge, which was able to take us all. In the morning – or, to be specific, 3 a.m. – there arrived a man with two sledges, and, after he had had something to eat, we loaded ourselves on. It was 10 January 1942 when we left this prison and threw ourselves out into the wide world.

AT LAST! LEAVING SIBERIA

We had an eiderdown, my mother and younger siblings sat on one of the sledges snuggled underneath it. Father, Janek and I walked behind the sledges, though the snow was heavy. At about lunchtime we reached the village of Szostowa, where in the summer I had worked in the woods for cash. We were there for about an hour. The driver gave the horses a rest and then we set off again as we had a long way to go. Before we left this village, I managed to sell some trousers which were padded with cotton wool, and for these I got a couple of loaves of rye bread. Then we set off through Czarom and other villages, right to the place where we were to get on a train. On the way I suddenly remembered that this was exactly the same road as the one on which we were taken when we were first brought to our settlement, Rzawki.

We passed many villages, and, as chance would have it, we even stayed overnight at the dwelling we had stayed at before. We arrived at this house and the landlady dealt with us in a very ordinary and unpleasant way, although she was one of the wealthiest people in the area. My brother and I decided to leave earlier in the morning and get a head start on the rest of the family, but because we did this we got lost and, as a consequence, we had to find somewhere to stay for the night. We stayed at a decent place where the landlord was very reasonable. In the morning we once again threw ourselves further on our journey and began asking where and how far was the stop at Kokszega. By the afternoon we limped into Kokszega and were reunited with our family. We had barely joined our family when Mother began to tell us what they had experienced. It was not until 2 a.m. the following morning that they had reached their destination, and Father had fallen ill on the journey.

Kokszega was a very small place, hopelessly inadequate and desperate. We stayed there for three days and nights before we started to load ourselves into the trains. While we stopped here we met a Polish lady who, during the First World War, had married a Russian commander. She had a young daughter and told us that she prayed to God when her husband or daughter was not looking – if they were looking she could not pray. In this place there were many Soviet prisoners who worked there and looked cold, dirty and dishevelled. At 2 a.m. we loaded ourselves on to the train, along with a man who had lived in our settlement and had three daughters. In the train we met two families from our village in Poland, who had been staying at a different settlement, and they began to tell us very frightening and moving accounts of what they had experienced. We went through the village of Wulsk during the day and by 10 a.m. we had reached the main station, Sinidze. There we got out and went into the waiting room, taking our belongings, which we still had with us.

This waiting room looked terrible as it was so tightly crammed with people; we were unable to walk from one end to the other. There was nowhere to sleep. Mother placed everything in the corner, sat my younger siblings on top and sat down herself to doze off. My father, brother and I had to manage how we could, dozing off on our feet, and this is how we spent one day after another. During the day it became a little easier because the people moved a little and there was more room. With regard to food, we received nothing as the ration books we had been using were not valid here.

The canteen and the food that was available was for those who worked at the station. As I was the eldest in the family it was my responsibility to organise something to drink, even if it was only some hot water; therefore I managed to find a landlady who allowed me to boil some water, but I had to pay her for this and it cost me more than just a little money. Father had some *machorke* (rough tobacco), so he took out a few packets and exchanged them for bread. In this way, we tried to save ourselves from death. We saw many Soviet prisoners who looked terrible, dirty and ragged. We stayed like this at the station for a week as it was impossible to get the train and it was even worse trying to get the tickets. The people would stand for two, three or even four days in a queue, waiting for their tickets. Somehow we had some luck when my brother went and after a long time, lost in the huge throng of people, he reached the ticket counter and paid 120 roubles for all our tickets. We got on to the train during the night.

The train was a passenger train, so crammed with prisoners that there was no room to move. It was made worse as they were all infested with lice and, as we were in such close proximity, we too became infested. We arrived in Vologda in the morning, and there we unloaded our belongings at the station; later we went to the waiting room. Because we had three very young brothers and sisters, Mother was able to go with the children to a separate waiting area, which was a lot better than the communal waiting area, if only because they were away from where the sad and pitiful prisoners were. I had travelled through so many parts of Russia and I had seen so many different villages and towns, but I had never seen such a place as here in Vologda and I am sure it will remain etched in my memory for the rest of my life. There were so many prisoners that it was difficult to keep an eye on our luggage, and it was difficult even to eat as they were capable of walking past and grabbing the food from our mouths.

It was freezing cold outside, and here and there we could see dead bodies lying on the ground. These were mainly tramps, beggars and those excluded from society; they had succumbed to the harsh realities. There was an occasion when we came through the doors just as one of them fell to the ground; no one took any notice that he was even lying there. The people just walked round and carried on their way. In the other communal waiting rooms it was even worse, and more bewildering. These poor people found themselves in dire circumstances. They had ripped and ragged clothes and no shoes, and badly bruised and broken skin, and, in addition to all this, they were suffering from starvation. They were dying all around us, but no one came to their aid.

One day I went with Mother, who had developed a rash on her arms, to the nurse, and she beckoned us into her office and dealt with us quite pleasantly. However, when one of the prisoners arrived, who could barely walk at all, one of the Soviet women pushed the prisoner away from the door and, as he had no strength, he fell to the floor. She then, with the Russian nurse, took him (one holding him by his feet and the other by his arms) and threw him on a large pile of bodies – those who had died only that night. In the morning, I saw two buses arrive to take away the bodies, and later they took away some of the prisoners who were still living – one was without a shirt; another was barefoot and had huge swollen feet. One after the other, they put them on the bus and took them somewhere. For a long time I could not erase these events from my memory. These revelations I could not forget: how people in Russia respect human beings and what communism is. If there had been a church, priests and faith in God, there would never have been so many excluded from society, and there would not be such terrible disrespect for human life by other humans. People can do terrible things to other people when they do not believe in God and when man does not know why he lives. Nowhere did I ever see such scenes again as those I saw during my time in Valogda.

The transport wagons for our train arrived in the afternoon and then my brother went with Father to prepare the carriage we were to travel in for our journey. They swept it, arranged the planks we were to sleep on and provided some heating so it would be warm. In the evening, we all moved off together to the carriage they had prepared. The carriage was not large; it was for heavy goods and it had a stove in the middle. We were to share it with a number of families. All were from the same part of Poland, called Sokal, apart from one family who were from Nowogrodka. We waited here another week until everyone had arrived and the train was ready to move on. There were just two carriages containing Poles, but there were four more which contained evacuees from Kiev and the Finnish borders.

In Valogda we received only 800 grams of bread per person each day and no more. Mother would boil black coffee on the stove, and we drank this alongside the heavily salted bread. I used to imagine at the time that if this bread had no salt, I would be able to eat it to my satisfaction. After the week was up we set off from Valogda.

The journey was horrendous. The train travelled so fast that it was impossible to boil anything on the stove – the carriage would jerk from side to side and the pans would fly into the air with everything they contained. Sometimes the train would stop at a large station where we were able to obtain bread and some soup, but there were times when the train tore along all day and night and sometimes just stopped in a secluded field and stayed this way for a long time, so we were unable to get anything. Because of this, we suffered badly from hunger and starvation, as well as from the cold as there was nowhere to get any firewood. We were given nothing, nothing at all, and we had to use our cunning to survive – and even steal as there was no other way.

After a few days of travelling like this, Father fell gravely ill. He was suffering with terrible pains in his back. He sat during the day and night in the carriage and groaned terribly. For three days, Father suffered in this terrible way and we looked on, not knowing how we could help him and not even able to give him anything to eat as we had nothing to spare and the train just kept going on and going on, non-stop.

Just before we reached the town of Swierdlowsk the train stopped and it was announced that it would be standing there a little longer than usual. The men, including my brother, left in order to try to find food from somewhere. We received some bread and soup – one portion per person. At this station we parted company from our father, and to this day we have had no news as to what might have happened to him.

A Russian doctor at this station went from carriage to carriage and checked if there was anyone ill. He saw Father and, after carrying out an examination, stated that he would have to be taken to hospital and remain there. There was no other remedy. It was then that we found ourselves without advice, and it was a critical situation. We were hesitant and frightened to leave our father alone; we could not help him and therefore we had to decide one way or another on how to save him. The doctor assured us that, once he had recovered, Father would be able to leave at any time and find us – maybe even catch us up on the journey. We therefore left everything to the will of God – whatever was to happen, let it happen. In about half an hour the sick were to leave us by train and travel to a hospital in the town of Swierdlowsk. My mother, my brother and I took Father to the train, which arrived after just over half an hour. There was quite a number of sick people, but of these there were only two Poles – Father and a boy. When the train arrived we led Father to it, said farewell, and the train left straight away.

I am saddened when I recall this moment because, at the time, I never thought that Father and I would never see each other again, that I would be saying farewell, goodbye to him for ever. I did not comprehend the significance of what was happening and what subsequently happened. When Father left, we reported back to our train, which had been standing some distance away from where we had parted from Father. When we arrived there, unfortunately the train had left a few minutes earlier and there were some sixty people left behind.

The discipline here was terrible. Passengers would leave the train, walk a few paces for water and would be left behind as no signals were given that the train was to start pulling away; no bells sounded to give a sign it was leaving. In this way, many people were split up from their families and were lost – nothing was heard of them again. There was great despair and anxiety when anyone left their carriage as no one knew how long the train would be standing or if it was going to set off again straight away, but people had to leave as there was nothing to eat – hunger and starvation forced us to leave the carriage. On this occasion, it was easier for us as there were sixty left behind, mainly Soviet mothers – evacuees torn away from their children. They went to the stationmaster and made such a fuss that he telephoned to Swierdlowsk and told them to hold up the train until we had caught up with it. He assured us that there would be a passenger train arriving within half an hour and that we would catch up with the train at Swierdlowsk.

The stationmaster predicted wrongly and a train only arrived for us after an hour and a half's wait at the station. The waiting was terrible – the frost was so cold that I froze, and I suffered because of this evening, just as my brother and mother did. When the train arrived it was only a few minutes before we were in Swierdlowsk. It was evening and therefore I could see very little of this town, but it must have been big as the station itself was so large that it took us quite a while to find our train, which was waiting for us. We only just managed to find it and get into our carriage before the train started to move off.

Again we travelled day after day. One day finished, another started and we lost track of what day it actually was. Poverty, misery and want began to weigh more heavily on us and our health got worse and began to fail.

A few days after we had become separated from our father, Mother fell ill with dysentery and she was writhing in agony. All day and night Mother suffered and we were helpless, without any knowledge of how we could ease her pain. There was nothing we could give her – nothing left to eat or drink which might have alleviated her agony even for one minute – so we offered up all our worries and hopes to the will of God; if God wanted it to happen, that is how it would be.

I remember the train stopping one day at a relatively small junction and, straight away, the commander on board and a few other people got out of the train in order to get something to eat – after all, we hadn't eaten since the previous morning. Our luck was in as we could see a canteen which was quite close where you could get some soup. This soup was cabbage soup – very bitter and quite runny – but no one took this into account. We didn't care what it looked like, just that we could have something that might nourish us.

The soup was shared out and everyone ate it as starvation had started taking hold. Even Mother, who was very ill, tired of all her agonies and completely drained of strength, started crying out for some of this soup which was very bitter like vinegar. Could I refuse my ill, suffering mother's wishes? I knew very well that this soup could be my mother's downfall and could lead her to her untimely death, as those who had dysentery had to stick to a strict diet, but I could not refuse her request. I whispered quietly to God, asking him not to abandon us at this critical time, hoping that he would not take our mother away from us as we would be left complete orphans as Father had already gone. If God took mother away from us, we would be left with no one to care for us. Although our mother at this time was ill and was unable to give us care, she gave us strength, and hardships were easier to bear just because of her being there – her presence with us.

Mother, after drinking some spoonfuls of this soup with such appetite as she had not shown for a long time, seemed to be transformed and it seemed as though she was ill no longer. On the following day, Mother's situation improved further; although she was still very weak and tired, all her pains had left her. I know for certain it was not the soup that had made my mother well, but that God did not want us to be orphaned yet. It was He who had returned Mother to health. We always prayed to Our Lady of Perpetual Succour for help and health, and therefore Our Lady granted us this wish through her Son. Mother regained her health, although not completely, and she was still with us. It was Our Lady of Perpetual Succour that we were grateful to, for her protection; without it, we would have disappeared with no trace.

We arrived at the town of Czelebinsk at around 10 a.m. I did notice that this town was quite pleasant. It was built up, with many factories, and it was the first town I had seen which looked nice. We found out that there were Poles billeted here, and therefore, when the train stopped, we started to look around to see whether we could meet someone who could give us some information. This was the first Polish outpost we had come across and from which we benefited. This was the first time we saw Polish soldiers. They came to our carriage and welcomed us in a pleasant manner. When this happened, tears welled up in our eyes – not because we had seen a soldier, but because we were leaving the Siberian Steppes and things had changed so much – we were now free. We could travel and we had a Polish army who would look after us. My memory at this time recalled what had been said to us at our settlement: "You will never see Poland again; it is for you to live and die here. Do not think that you will ever return to Poland as there will never be a Poland." The commander back at the settlement would repeat this to us over and over again, but despite this we all lived in the hope that we would not remain there for ever and that we would be vindicated. However, there were very many who died there and did not have their hopes and dreams fulfilled. This Polish soldier who stood before us rekindled our hopes and dreams as if awakening us, giving us better hope, telling us to believe that we would not disappear as we had already got this far. These Polish outposts, which we were to pass through on many occasions, would help us to carry on; each of them was like an oasis in so many different ways, and they gave us all we needed. The soldier took with him a couple of our men and gave them some bread from their stores, a variety of other products and 20 roubles for each of the larger families. What they gave us lasted a couple of days.

We were travelling for a long time, and everyone by now was exhausted and could barely stand on their legs. On our journey we often came across canteens where you could buy something to eat, but nowhere did the train stop for any length of time. At one such stop the train pulled up right in front of the canteen and everyone quickly jumped out to get some soup; the train was very close to the canteen – only a few paces away from our carriage. I was not dressed very well and was wearing no layers to fight the cold as I was sure that at any moment I would be able to jump back into the carriage before the train could pull away. It was almost my turn for the soup when the whistle on the train blew and it started to leave. There were five of us still outside.

The train was already travelling fast, but, with the various plates and bowls we were carrying, we managed to jump and, as if by some miracle, scramble on to one of the carriages which carried coal. To this day I will never forget just how much I froze on this occasion. The train, as if to make matters even worse, thundered along without stopping, hour after hour. We huddled together, side by side, practically frozen stiff, just waiting and looking forward either to the train stopping or to our dying like this – it made no difference to us. When the train did eventually stop I was unable to get out of the carriage. I had frozen that much. When I finally got to my carriage, Mother laid me down, covered me with the eiderdown and gave me some hot coffee to warm me up; it was only after some two hours that I started to recover and come back to myself. I never fully recovered from this ordeal, and from this time onward my health began to fail me.

Another time, when it was nearly afternoon and I was already not well, the train stopped and I went for some water, carrying a bucket. I had barely reached the well when the whistle blew and the train moved off. There was no way I could reach my carriage as I was quite a way off and, therefore, one of the Soviet evacuees, who obviously had a heart, started shouting to me to hold my hands up and she would pull me aboard; otherwise I would be left behind. Although the train was travelling fast, I reached out with my hands and she pulled me aboard, along with someone else. This time, however, I really had overdone it and I became very ill. For a couple of days I had a very high temperature and I could not move – not even from my plank bed. The sun was warmly beating down against the carriage doors as we had now travelled a long way south.

WARMER CLIMES

It was Arys, in Kazakhstan, when the train finally stopped, and this day will always remain firmly etched in my memory. When they opened the doors to the carriage, the sun was beating down warmly; no snow could be seen anywhere. I lay there with a very high temperature, my head splitting, in unbelievable pain. Almost immediately, a nurse appeared wearing an army uniform and, after taking my temperature, she informed us that I should be taken to hospital and if I were unable to get there myself, they would arrange for a stretcher and someone to take me there. I started crying and the nurse started to comfort me and calm me down, saying that once I had recovered from my illness I would be able to return to my family. My mother helped me to get dressed and she placed 20 roubles in my handbag. I said goodbye to my family, and my brother and another girl took me under the arm and led me to a building which seemed like a waiting room. Here they laid me on a sofa and made me comfortable. After a few minutes something which looked like a stretcher on two wheels arrived and I was taken to another building. This was not the hospital but a room which held the sick, lying there in their clothes and not even washed. My brother Janek accompanied me the whole way and promised me that he would visit me on the next day as he knew where I was. The day was 28 January 1942.

On the next day, very early in the morning, before my

brother had come, there arrived transport for me, and one of the nursing sisters led me out. These were not our Polish nurses but Soviet nurses. She made me comfortable in the taxi and took me to the hospital, which was some way away from the town. On the journey I kept looking up to try to see where we were going, to try to remember the journey so that when it came to return from the hospital after my recovery I would know the way. It was a difficult task and my efforts were to no avail. All I could remember was that the hospital was a long way away from the station. When we arrived at the hospital, the nursing sister helped me climb out of the taxi and helped me into the middle of a wide corridor in the hospital.

The hospital was a very large one, comprising two buildings. As I walked along the corridor it seemed to me that I was completely healthy and nothing was hurting me. When the nursing sister came to measure my temperature it was good at 38.2 degrees and she wanted to leave me as the temperature was not high. After the third reading, she told all the other nurses to leave me. It was then that my temperature rocketed. The nurse who had brought me there led me further down the main corridor and put me on a bench by the wall. On this bare bench, without anything to cover me, I lay until the evening with my thoughts telling me that this was maybe the end of me – I would die before they could find a bed for me to lie on. In the evening, when all the lights were on, I was taken for a bath and I froze even more, almost to freezing point.

The water was not warm. It was so cold that by the time the nurses had washed me and cut my hair I was shaking, completely out of control with fever.

They took my clothes to be disinfected and did not allow me to keep my handbag, in which I had my 20 roubles and my prayer book. I received a nightshirt, a scarf for my head and a very thin blanket. There was no bed available, but all the way down the corridor wooden planks had been placed by the wall on both sides; these were the sleeping arrangements. This is where they put me. They immediately brought me my supper, but I did not feel like eating anything. I felt extremely cold, with the fever and high temperature sapping my strength. I had a terrible night. I could not sleep because I was so cold, freezing to the bone so much so that in the morning, when I saw the sister and the doctor, I remember shouting at them in an animal-like voice, a voice which was not human, to take me away from there to somewhere warmer as I was freezing. They took very little notice; they were not interested at all in my plight. At that time I lost my memory and consciousness of my surrouondings. All I do remember clearly was that it was cold. I ate nothing. I became deaf like a tree stump. There was no medicine, and no one, not even a doctor, came to see me all day. I remember a nurse giving me some kind of card; I looked at it and did not know what it was. It was only later when I started to regain my memory and my consciousness that I read the card. It was written by my brother Janek, who was in Taszkent. I read it over and over again, and then remembered and realised the full reality.

On the second night, sometime after midnight, I was eventually moved into one of the smaller rooms, which had one window. I was placed on a bed and, at last, I received another blanket, which I could use to cover myself better. I lay there surrounded by Soviet women who were ill too and, just like me, suffering from typhus. I lay like this for a few days without memory, and the majority of time I slept, occasionally waking up and always finding food by my bed. While I was very ill the food was acceptable. In the mornings they gave me milk in a very small cup and a small amount of butter and later some miserable-looking, poor-quality bread, about 200 grams a day. For a few days I was unable to feed myself and a Soviet nurse helped me. I never ate all this food, but when my health started to return, and my temperature fell, my fever left me and I started to feel my hunger. I suffered hunger pains.

I remember one time when a Polish nurse came to visit. She came to me with the Russian female doctor, who was very pleasant and had looked after me while I was very ill. The doctor talked to the Polish nurse and explained that I was not eating. I remember the Polish nurse telling the doctor that she would have left me some cocoa, but because I was not eating she decided not to leave any. She said she would leave some the next time. I later had regrets that I had not taken this small box of cocoa, as on the second day my appetite had returned, along with my consciousness. I felt and looked terrible as the food rations were very small and of poor quality, and I suffered terrible hunger. Despite all this I did feel a lot better than I had done and I was at least able to walk around my bed.

How terrible these days were for me! While I lay on my bed unconscious of my surroundings, with no memory, I was unable to think, but as soon as my consciousness returned, the reality stood there in front of my eyes and I was overwhelmed with fright that I was on my own, without Mother and without my family. I had only my own counsel to rely on for the immediate future, and I had to defend myself from death and somehow get back to my family. I was not sure if I would be able to find them again. It was these thoughts that passed through my mind and acted like a death blow; these thoughts were what tormented me, and I found it unbearable to think about what would happen once I left hospital. It was not good in hospital, and starvation continued to rack my body, but they did at least give me something to eat; I didn't know how I would survive once I was released. It is difficult for me to recall this time, but it is firmly etched in my memory. The day came when at last I had to leave hospital. By the end of the day the female doctor confirmed that the next day, which was 13 February 1942, I would be leaving hospital. Up until this time I had not been anywhere and I was unable to walk at all, but as soon as I heard I was to leave hospital I had to gather all my strength and get my legs working.

On 13 February 1942 I received no food at all, and at 9 a.m. I was led to the hall I had seen when I arrived. There I had to have a bath, but this time I was not there long and I quickly washed myself. They returned to me the clothes which had been taken away when I arrived. I wept in despair when I looked into my purse, which had been placed inside my shoe, and the 20 roubles my mother had given me when we parted was not there. All my shouting and lamenting did not help; no one returned it to me. I was left then without hope, my strength drained, helpless and powerless. These few roubles would have lasted me at least two days, but they had stolen them from me and I was left with nothing – even the socks I had brought with me had been taken. At 12 p.m. I received confirmation from the hospital that I was leaving and a nurse led me to the gates. Without strength and feeling very weak, I did not know what I should do with myself.

I cried incessantly until the people who were walking past began to ask me what I wanted and why I was crying. When I came to my senses and realised where I was, I knew I could not behave in this way. It was important that somehow I had to rescue myself and help myself, in any way possible, so I began to walk ahead! What I must have looked like I do not know. Every time I took one step it appeared to me that I had fallen down a big hole, and I had to stop frequently as darkness kept falling over my eyes. I met many people on this road, but there was no one who was able to tell me whether I was taking the correct road to the railway station. With the help of God, I managed to reach the station; there I met Polish people who were serving in the army and, straight away, I was able to turn to them for help and information.

There were two ladies and two men eating and they offered to share their food with me; as I had not eaten anything all day, I was grateful even for a small piece of bread. They told me the road I should take which would lead me to the Polish outpost where they were billeted. It was some distance away from the town and I reached it by late afternoon. I met many people there who were waiting in a queue to see the officials, and I also had to wait in this queue even though I was very weak. The delegate who was there listened to my story and confirmed that I would be placed on any train going through so that I could go after my family. He gave me 20 roubles, 800 grams of bread, 100 grams of sugar, a little tea, 300 grams of semolina and 200 grams of sausage. All this food was a great feast for a person as starved as I was! I returned to the station and there I was shown into one of the carriages with people who were complete strangers to me.

Two of the ladies in this carriage told me they had gone for soup and, when they had returned to their train, it had left with their children on board. One of the ladies had left two children: a three-year-old and a five-year-old. The other had left four children, the youngest being seven years old. These ladies paced about the carriage as if they had lost their minds; they did not know what to do with themselves. I also met a couple of men who had become separated from their families like the two women, and they had nothing, not even their hats! One of them was from our parish in Poland and his loss was even greater and worse than others as he had become separated from the train in Walogda and had not seen his family since. He looked terrible and had wasted away so much that I would never have recognised him had he not told me where he was from – what can happen to people, and even people so young!

In the carriage there was no room on the plank beds as they were occupied by families, and therefore I had to sleep lower down, at the very bottom. Many a time I suffered from the cold as I had nothing to cover myself with, except the coat I was wearing. These were very hard times I lived through. During the day I was tormented by hunger and at night by the extreme cold. We departed on 16 March 1942 from Arys in the direction of Taszkent, and this is the direction I had to take as I knew that my family had travelled there.

By the end of the day we had reached Taszkent and I noticed that our carriage had been unhooked from the main train and was awaiting repairs. In the morning the men had organised themselves to find the Polish outpost which was in the town. Dysentery had broken out and we were forbidden to enter certain areas. Purely by accident, we met a delegate from the army, but he told us he was unable to help. The only thing he said he could give us was a little soap and a few roubles. Subsequently, in the afternoon, he brought us a small bar of soap and 30 roubles each – but what good was this? There was nothing to buy. We waited there for three days and we suffered terribly with hunger.

I looked like a shadow of my former self and so I took myself off to do some begging. I am filled with grief, sadness and sorrow when I remind myself of these times, but it is completely true: I went from house to house begging for a piece of bread. On the first day I was quite successful and I collected quite a few pieces – so many that I was able to have some for supper and leave a small piece for breakfast. On the second day, I was unable to get anything and I met many people who even laughed at me. There was, however, one lady who did give me a piece of bread and, as she turned away, she spoke to me and said in Russian to pray for her daughter who had died, if I had any faith in God.

On the third day we left Taszkent having had barely anything to eat. We arrived at a station (I cannot remember its name) when it was already night and we stopped here for quite some time. We met many of our beloved soldiers, who were guarding a large grain store. Besides the soldiers there were also a couple of night watchmen guarding the grain. We were successful in getting the attention of one of the night watchmen and managed to get him to come out to our carriage on the pretence of selling him some woollen boots. We started our negotiations with him in the far corner of our carriage. We sat him down on a log of wood with his back towards the door. As he negotiated for the boots, we left, one by one, to gather some of the grains of wheat – not a lot, but just enough. We brought this back to our carriage where the night watchman continued to negotiate. Shortly after this escapade, we travelled on, and at least we now had this little bit of grain in our store. In the morning, as the train sped on, I roasted the grains of wheat in a metal box, which had previously held tinned food, and this is how we kept ourselves alive.

We passed many stations and, as we travelled, the misery and heat worsened. There were now fewer Polish outposts where we might get help, and the outposts we did find were unable to offer us anything. To add to our misery we saw that, on many occasions, the Jewish people were accepted before us, but we were unable to find anyone who would give us support. Under these circumstances, we were left with no alternative but to watch from the side and see what would happen next.

We eventually arrived at our last station, which was Tergany. There we were to unload and go to one of the collective farms. First thing in the morning two Polish representatives came to our carriage. They looked after Polish affairs in Tergany, and they told us the situation with the people who were in the collective farms – they said that there was nothing to eat and misery reigned everywhere. They advised us to make our way to a town called Gorczakow, where the army was based – and this is what we did. If we could register with the army, maybe we would have the luck of getting away abroad; otherwise we would perish.

There were so many people in our carriage who were ill. They were taken to the hospital in Tergany, and after a couple of days we made our way on foot to Gorczakow on 10 April 1942. The distance from Tergany was eight kilometres, but we had become accustomed to anything and this journey seemed like nothing compared to some of the journeys we had already made. When we arrived, we found many tents had been pitched and there was no lack of people. By the time we had settled in and assessed the situation, it appeared we had arrived a little late as the transport going abroad had left on 28 March and the second transport was now being put together. It was envisaged that it would be ready towards the end of April.

I went to the office where volunteers for the army were registering, to see if I could find anything out about my brother, but nothing came of it. I did not know where my family was and where my brother might be. Was he in the army or not? There was no mention of him at all, and therefore I was unable to register myself and I remained a civilian. No luck came my way and I was unable and unwilling to lie. At each step I wanted to cry; I wanted my family, my mother, and I had no idea where to go and get help and information. Dark thoughts and grief surrounded me. The officials started differentiating between families of army personnel and those who were civilians in a whole variety of ways.

On one particular occasion a corporal visited my tent. He was quite old. At this moment I do not remember his name, but he told me that all civilians must leave their tents and gather in a place outside and anyone who did not do so of their own free will would be forcibly removed. To me this was a terrible blow, and to this day I do not know who gave this order, but it was carried out. From this time onwards, whenever this particular corporal made his visits to the tents, I made a point of going out and not being there. One day I returned after one of his visits and found that my 'sleeping pallet' had been moved outside the tent. I started weeping uncontrollably. The commander of this tent stated that he had had to do this; he had no choice. After considering all the factors, I believe that the Jewish family who slept opposite me had brought on my downfall. I was taken in by a lady I knew from the tent next to ours, and there I found a sleeping area in the middle of the tent as there was no room anywhere else. This lady had not registered yet either, and she had just got out of hospital, so we agreed between ourselves that I would register myself as her sister – not of the same father, but the same mother. The plan would have worked, but luck did not come my way and I did not know how to lie. When I was registering I was asked by the army personnel – who knew me well as I had been trying to find my brother through them several times – what my mother's name was, and I said Eva. He then asked the girl with me what her mother's name was and she said Maria. Then he said that if one mother was Eva and the other Maria, how could we be from the same mother? I left in tears. It seemed to me that there was no longer a reason for me to live in this world; but God remembers about everyone, and He would remember me. I did not look for another occasion to register as part of a family which served in the army, but I left my situation to the will of God. What God wants, let it happen.

One evening, I was walking through the area and I met someone whom I knew, although not very well. Her name was Stefa Klimek from Stanislawow. I had met her on only two occasions in Poland, although Father had on many occasions spoken about her father and regarded them as our friends from the west of Poland. When I had introduced myself to her and got to know her better, she introduced me to her family and I said to them that I would like to join them in order that I would have people I could trust in the event of something happening to me. At that particular time there was no room in their tent, but, after a couple of days, several people were taken away to the hospital, which then enabled me to move into their places. We did not live in this tent for very much longer. There was no transport going out of the country, so any transport which became available was being used by the army as they were leaving Guzar. We therefore had no reason to stay in this place except for survival.

We were receiving 400 grams bread each per day and soup, when it was left over from the army. Those who had some money were at least able to buy some flour for themselves, even though a kilogram cost between 60 and 70 roubles. I had to live on *makochem* which is pressed vegetables, dry, hard and mainly eaten by animals. I also ate nettles, which were quite difficult to collect as everyone was trying to do the same and only very small amounts were left. It was announced that we would all be dispersed into various kolkhozy as the army was leaving. There would, for the time being at least, be no transport abroad. We all started crying and lamenting over our misfortune, but things did reach a conclusion.

On 15 May 1942 some carts pulled by oxen arrived; two were quite high and had two wheels. We registered ourselves not far from where we were staying, which was the Taszkent region, about eight kilometres away. We arrived there in the evening, and as there was no room for us they made some space in the tea room. There we slept on the carpet for a few nights, until they found us a room. The rooms we were allocated were in a shack and looked awful. The shack was low with a clay roof, which was flat. It had two rooms. In one there lived an Uzbek, with his wife and three children; the oldest girl's name was Michadzil, the boy's name was Hadziatham and the youngest girl's name I cannot remember. In our room the walls were as black as soot and on the wall, instead of a window, there were three holes which the light came through during the day. On these black walls were imprints of white hands, which the Russian lady told us had been made by some Poles who had lived here before us. On the floor we arranged our bedding, which consisted of straw and cotton wool. Occasionally, we would take our bedding outside because it was unbelievably hot in the hut.

At first we were not chased out to do any work, but, by the same measure, we were not given anything to eat. After five days they gave us 400 grams of wheat per person, but beyond that nothing. What we received from our friends and what we had been given at Gorczakow when we set off – a kilogram of flour and some canned meat – was all we had, and soon it was nearly all eaten, although we ate in a way that made it seem to us as if nothing had been consumed. The flour we received was only good for making the soup thicker. Hunger once again began to torment us more and more, and the grass we were eating was becoming more and more inedible. Occasionally we would gather wild berries, which were not very appetising, and boil these to make a kind of soup, which we would thicken with flour, but we had no bread at all. We took the wheat we had been given to the mill to be ground, and that is how we lived. Why they gave us nothing for twenty days I do not know. Dark nights and despair began to embrace us. We did not go to work, and in this putrid, smelly, infested hut it was unbearable.

At this time I had 30 roubles, which I had received when we left our previous settlement, so I bought some *makochem* and, occasionally, half a glass of milk (as a full glass cost 2 roubles) and I would make pancakes. I would also go and pick the wild apples which grew in the fields, and that is how I lived. This lack of nourishment dried me out to such an extent that I soon could not walk, and, besides that, it had ruined my stomach.

After twenty days they gave us a sheaf of barley which was still green. When we saw this we all started crying, and the man who had given out the sheaves of barley stated, "If an Uzbek can eat them, you can eat them too."

We took the sheaves of barley, and the Uzbek told us how we should prepare them. To start, we had to break off the ears of barley, dry these out in the sun and then beat them until all that was left were the grains of clean barley. These would then be tipped into a cauldron, which was continually kept on the fire. The grains would then be well fried and pulped into porridge. Slowly but surely, we learnt everything we needed to know, and later we were able to adapt our skills to live – and to live for something.

The worst period in the year was the period leading up to the harvest; as soon as the wheat appeared on the stalks and started ripening, things became easier. We then started to go and steal the crops for food. This was generally done during the night, and the food made us feel better, although our stomachs would sometimes not accept the food as our insides had already been badly damaged by the *makochem* and grass. We went to steal tomatoes, watermelons, melons, wild berries, onions and whatever we could, but there were times when this activity could have put us into deep trouble.

When harvest arrived we were not allowed to take anything. We had to go and gather wheat and barley, but I never saw any rye and oats being grown anywhere. As we did the harvesting we always had with us a small bag and, naturally, in this bag we always put something, whether it was ears of the cereal we were picking or the crushed grains themselves. We never went back home with our 'beggar's bag' empty; there was always something we had gathered, and we kept our small bags with us and filled them wherever and whenever an opportunity presented itself.

I remember one occasion when the wheat was on the stalks (wheat was harvested twice a year). We had been tasked with planting beetroot with our co-workers, who were Jewish evacuees from Kiev, and we were working together without any Uzbeks supervising us; but there was a Jewish brigadier in charge, and his wife also worked with us. We made an arrangement with him that we would go into the wheat field and gather some wheat for ourselves. He would act as a lookout and if he saw anyone he would whistle, whereupon we would disperse as quickly as possible so no one would see us. So that is what happened. A whole gang of us made a hit on the wheat field, and, as fast as we could, we started to fill our bags with grain. After about twenty minutes of this manic activity, we heard a whistle and, like birds, we scattered from the field and hid in the bushes, of which there were many. After some time we all got back together again and began to ask what or whom the brigadier had seen. As it transpired, he had seen nothing, but it seemed to him that we had been too long already doing our 'harvesting' and that was why he had whistled. All was well, however, as we had picked enough to last us. It was hard to carry all this grain home with us, but somehow luck was with us, and we managed.

We always prayed for God's protection and, just like the thieves who pray that their mission is a success, we prayed so intently that we would not only be protected when we stole the grain, but also that we would get it to our homes where it was safer. Fortunately, the Uzbeks took little notice of our escapades as they had previously done the same, only on a much greater scale. There was no flour mill in our area, so we had to go to a neighbouring one. Sometimes we had to sit and wait all night and we also had to contend with chasing off and arguing with the Uzbeks there. The Uzbeks would pester us terribly and they had no respect at all for women, particularly if they were defenceless. For this reason it was dangerous, even during the day, to go anywhere on our own.

The flour mill only had one stone and was water-driven, with the grain being milled only once, which left it quite coarse and bulky. There were many occasions when fighting broke out between ourselves and the Uzbeks as they would not allow us to use the mill, but would leave us waiting there, longer and longer. During the three months and a few days we had been there we tried to live, work and cooperate with the Uzbeks; however, if we had stopped there any longer, I cannot imagine what the consequences might have been, but God and Our Lady had not forgotten us.

One evening as we sat, thinking about when our departure abroad would happen, a lady from Taszkent appeared. She had visited several other kolkhozy and she told us that our departure was scheduled for around 15 August. She added that it might be a good idea to go to the village square and find out more, and also to see what was going on there and whether any produce was for sale. On the next day, I went with my friend Stefa Krupa, and as we were walking we noticed a queue, so we decided to join it with our bags – maybe they were giving something away or maybe there was something to take. Of course, when we got to the front we found out that registrations were taking place, but only for those who had family in the army. As I had no proof, I made my way to a man called Lieutenant Czastkiewicz, who was doing the administration there. He showed great interest in my case and told me that he would write out a certificate to confirm that I had a brother who was in the army; I would then be able to register as a member of an army family. I would be able to board the transport going abroad and eventually complete my quest of finding my family. Naturally, I did not know how to thank the lieutenant enough for his kindness as I had tried so hard in the past, and in so many different ways, to be registered as someone who had a member of their family in the Polish Army. Now, finally, I had received my wish. I went with Stefa, carrying this small and seemingly insignificant piece of paper that was so incredibly important, to the office for registration, and we registered ourselves. We later went to the warehouse for some provisions, which they were giving out to take back to the camp. This time they gave us quite a lot of produce, and a man who had previously travelled in the same carriage as us began to laugh at my expense. He said I should eat as much as I could now because if I ever ran short of food during the journey he would look after me and give me some more. I cannot describe the happiness which reigned among all the Poles. The only thing that anyone talked about was our impending journey abroad, although no one was certain when this would happen. We started returning to our kolkhoz late in the evening and were frightened that the Uzbeks would attack us, steal our possessions and brutally beat us.

We arrived at our hut feeling very tired as it was very late in the evening, but no one was asleep yet. We related to everyone what we had found out and they were all delighted. The next day, we went to work as usual, with the exception of Stefa, who stayed behind to visit her mother, who was in hospital, to take her something to eat and to inform her of our impending journey out of the country.

A woman named Klimek, who hailed from Sokola and also nearby Bochnia at a place called Ostrowa, was not all that old, but she seemed elderly. The life we led had taken its toll and made us all look older. Her legs had swollen and the poor lady could not walk, and towards the end she actually kept saying that she would not leave here as she felt she was going to die. That is what happened a week before our departure: she died in hospital.

Transport was provided, so her body could be brought to the camp, and there, in a small cemetery where there were only a few graves, she was buried in holy memory. How awful this funeral looked! The grave which was dug was shallow and there was no coffin. We took the body, which was covered in cloth, by the head and feet and placed it in the grave, on top of some branches. We did the burial as no one else was with us – there was no one to help. The Uzbek who had brought the body disappeared straight back to town. We covered the grave with soil so it was slightly raised and placed a wooden cross as a marker. The grave was then 'decorated' with thorns in order to keep the jackals off.

The Uzbeks buried their dead in a different way, with the deceased in a sitting position, without a coffin, and it was only the men that went to the funeral. The women, before the sun went down, were in their houses wailing and lamenting loudly. This could be heard from one hut to another and it is also believed that this wailing went on when their menfolk were sent to fight at the front. The wailing would go on not for one or two days, but for two to three weeks.

Time went by quickly, and in the evenings we always went to the neighbouring camp to find out if a date had been fixed. At last, we found out that on 20 August all the Poles were to gather in the town square, as the departure abroad was to go ahead on 25 August. There was so much happiness, and it is impossible to put into words what we were feeling at that time.

We began to prepare ourselves for the journey. I had no bag with me, but with the help of my good friends I used a piece of sackcloth to make myself a knapsack. In this, I could place the few clothes I had, which had been given to me by other good people. I also made a small case in which I was able to place some food and my documents, and that was all. We received our pay for all the time we had spent at the camp (this amounted to 150 roubles) and three kilograms of grain for our journey. A horse and cart was allocated to take us to the town square. On 20 August at 9 a.m. we loaded our possessions on to the cart. To one side, looking on, were the Jews from Kiev who had fled from the German bombings. The Jewish ladies were crying because we were leaving and we would have a better life somewhere else, where there was white bread. One young girl said this to her mother: "Why am I Jewish? If I was not, I would be able to go with the Poles." We took very little notice of this, but would occasionally pass them some words of encouragement.

Within the hour, our transport departed and we were on our way. Jędryk, and Gienka, as we agreed, would travel on the horse and cart with the Uzbek to keep an eye on him and our belongings. Stefa, Hela, and I would walk to Gorczakow. It was late afternoon by the time we reached our destination, and the sun was beating down mercilessly. In the village square there was a building and next to this was a huge orchard with trees of fruit, including wild berries, peaches and small plums. In the shade of the trees there were many families already gathered, some known to us and some unknown. We found a place in the shade under a tree with wild berries. After some time, the horse and cart arrived with our belongings and we began to unload our things.

I was in despair as I could not find my knapsack. I started to cry loudly as I had nothing left except the clothes I stood in – no change of clothes, no underwear, nothing to cover myself with during the night. I did, however, still have my little case which I called my 'small chicken hut', as it looked just like one with two small doors on the side – this was all I had. It was lucky that this too had not disappeared as it contained my documents. My girlfriends started to cheer me up. We were leaving this country and, as for sleeping, to keep warm I could share a bunk with one of them. What else could I do? I resigned myself to the will of God. During the night I shared a bed with Stefa, and this I did each night until we reached Krasnowodsk.

The next day we went to Taszkent to do some shopping. I had acquired some sort of meat stock – I was not sure whether it was lamb or beef – but as it turned out to be totally unusable, during the journey, I had to throw it away.

We also bought some chicken for 60 roubles. As you can see, towards the end of our stay we were beginning to spoil ourselves with some of the better things in life; however, our already ruined stomachs were unable to accept all this food. As soon as we arrived back from Taszkent, the chicken was boiled and we had something else prepared for eating. On the third day, which was 23 August, it was announced that we should not stray anywhere as the officials would be checking our things to find out what we were taking with us. That afternoon they started their checks; duvets were not allowed to be taken, neither were furs, and they confiscated a lot of other things – we were to travel as lightly as possible. After their rummaging and checking, they moved us to another place, and on 24 August we all went to have a bath in readiness for our journey. The person in charge of the operation (I cannot remember his name – quite a thickset, energetic man who wound his way among the families) was recommending that everyone should try to buy whatever fruit they could get; he recommended grapes and watermelon, of which there was an abundance. He went on to say that should anyone become ill during the journey they would be left behind at the nearest hospital. The officials announced that at midnight that day they were going to start to read out the lists of who was to go on the transport, and they told us that not everyone was going to leave. Three hundred families were to remain behind as there was inadequate space due to the arrival of fewer carriages than expected. We were shaking in terror with anticipation, waiting for the moment when our names would be read out and we would know whether we were included in the list and on the journey. We could not sleep that evening and we talked about what would happen if we were not on the list or if one of us was excluded. At last, midnight arrived and they started to read out the prepared list of names. Everyone listened attentively and some were more impatient than others; no one wanted to be one of the 300 families left behind.

After a long wait, our names were read out. We were overcome with emotion and started to hug and kiss one another, crying with joy. Some families were crying that they were going, while others were crying because they were not going, and trouble began from the families who had been excluded.

Straight after our names were read out, although it was already dark, we took our belongings and made our way to the station, which was about a kilometre away from the town square. Other families were also making their way down to the station, including many who had not had their names read out and obviously were not supposed to go. There we gathered and, at the last table on the platform, our documents would be checked. They took our authorisation cards and our Polish soldiers escorted us to our carriages. Our group, luckily, all managed to keep together and we were escorted to our carriage – carriage number fourteen. We felt great happiness and relief as we at last found ourselves on a train with the certainty that we were going to leave this country and travel somewhere where there would be white bread! The carriage was not packed with people, and I cannot understand, to this day, why 300 families had to be left behind. It remains a mystery. A family consisting of a mother and two daughters had their names read out; but when they went to have their documents and certificate confirmed at the station by the NKVD, one daughter and the mother were crossed off the list, but the other daughter remained. That is how they left – they were split up.

The Jews at Gorczakow were not being evacuated with us, but they had been informed that there would be another transport arriving to collect them, and to this day they are still waiting to go. An order had been given that no Jew was to leave to go abroad as they had chosen, by their own free will, to travel to Russia. On the last day, I witnessed the following incident in the square. One lady came to the man who was reading out the list of families who were to leave and asked him if she had been included in the list of people leaving. Lieutenant Czastkiewicz, who was standing nearby, looked at her and said, "What is your name?" and when she replied, he said this to her, "Please find this lady on the list and immediately cross her name out. This lady is a Jew – I can identify her by her nose." The lady started to lament and cry, but nothing she did was able to change anybody's mind and at the last minute her name was crossed off the list. Although at Gorczakow the authorities were very strict with the Jews, I saw and met many beyond the borders of this country who wore medals, and many who even wore a crucifix. At 8 a.m. our train set off from the station to Krasnowodsk. It was 25 August 1942.

My mother's diary ends here.

EPILOGUE

My mother did eventually catch up and rejoin her mother, sisters and brothers. The train arrived and she travelled to Krasnowodsk, which is on the coast of the Caspian Sea. From here her journey continued across the Caspian Sea to Pahlevi. My mother spoke about this journey many times. It was one of the worst journeys she had ever been on as they had to sail through a storm. After a short quarantine period in Pahlevi, Mother travelled to Teheran, where she was reunited with her family.

From Teheran, the family travelled to Ahwaz and then to Isfahan. An infrastructure had been built here of schools, shops, workshops and a Polish Administration Sector had been set up. My mother worked as a dressmaker, as she had already completed her education in Poland. In 1943 the family left Isfahan and travelled to Karachi, where they stayed about six months.

My mother in Isfahan.

From here they boarded a ship and sailed to Bombay (now Mumbai).

When they arrived in Bombay they were moved, along with many thousands of Polish families, to a camp for mothers and their children, called Valivade, in the state of Kolhapur. It was here that my mother recounted her memories and wrote them down, providing a permanent record of what she had endured in the USSR.

The way the Polish families were living in India was heavenly bliss compared to how they had recently been living, and what they had endured in Siberia. Food was available and the ever present threat of starvation had been lifted. The climate was warm and all the Polish children thrived here. My mother and her family lived for five years in India and in 1948 they completed the final leg of the journey. They sailed from Bombay, across the Indian Ocean, through the Suez Canal into the Mediterranean Sea to Gibraltar, and finally reached their destination at Southampton in April 1948.

The ship that brought my family from Bombay to Southampton, arriving in April 1948.

Poles arriving at Southampton were placed in transit camps in Sussex and Surrey. From there they were dispersed to civilian camps dotted all over the UK. My mother and family went to Lincolnshire. Here, my mother's mother (my grandmother) met up with a lady she had known from Poland, who had also been forced on the rough journey through the USSR. This lady introduced my mother to her son, my future father. They were married in 1949 and now a different journey started – a journey together with my father. They raised five children and moved house on a number of occasions before eventually settling down.

My mother's mother.

Life was very difficult at the beginning, as it was for all Polish families, because they had arrived in this country with nothing. My father worked as a miner in the coalfields in Pontefract and Hemsworth. My mother never agreed with Father working in the mines as she did not want him exposing himself to danger every day when he had young children at home. Before long they moved to Bradford, where father worked first in textiles and then for an engineering firm. It was about this time that I was born, followed by my younger brother, which made the family complete.

My parents had always wanted to live away from the city, and with a large family it made sense to move out to the

My mother and father, outside the church on their wedding day, 1949.

countryside; so this is what they did. In 1957 my father purchased a smallholding on the outskirts of Queensbury. This smallholding was not too big, but it was sufficient to provide us all with fresh vegetables, eggs, milk and cheese and it was an abundant playground for the children. I always fondly remember my childhood years spent here as we were able to roam about, making as much noise as we liked, without any neighbours banging on our walls or telling us to be quiet. The air was fresh and we were seldom ill. We lived at one of the highest locations in Bradford, with a wonderful view of the whole city.

My father would work and my mother would take care of the children and tend to the smallholding. The family house would always be open for any family, friends or acquaintances to visit and they would be given some of our homemade cheese, which in time became a very sought-after commodity among members of the Polish community in Bradford.

Mother would grow a whole variety of vegetables and fruit, including strawberries, gooseberries and lots of rhubarb. As it was such a large garden, I remember helping my father turn the soil in preparation for the next planting.

My parents lived here from 1957 to 1995, when they decided it was time to downsize as all their children had married and moved out to start their own families. In 1997 my father passed away and then Mother left this world in 2005.

It was at this time that I had the opportunity to read my mother's writings, which described in some detail her time spent in the USSR, and it gave me a better understanding of my mother's life. I started to appreciate even more what she had endured and how this had moulded her as a person.

I remember very early on, when we had moved to our house high on the hills of Queensbury, that my mother would hoard dry bread in a huge plastic bag. I remember asking her why she was doing this and I remember her reply: "There

From left to right:
Mother, Irene, Father's mother, Stan, Mother's mother, Maria, Father
and kneeling, Zbigniew my youngest brother, and me.

My mother and father at my sister's wedding in 1977.

might not be any fresh bread tomorrow!" The skills she had acquired, such as mushroom-picking and berry-picking, were put to good use. One of her first enquiries when we moved was "Where are the nearest woods?" I remember the first time we went to these woods – we collected so many mushrooms we could barely carry them home. My mother had collected more than any of us, and how wonderfully tasty they were!

My mother was a very social person. She loved to be surrounded by her family and to be in the company of people. We enjoyed many family occasions, which today are not quite as frequent as they used to be. When her family responsibilities declined, Mother began to visit the sick, the infirm and the dying in the Polish parish in Bradford, through the organisation Caritas.

From left to right: Zosia, Jozefa, Janek, Tadek, Wladek, Marysia.
Foreground: Uncle Janek's wife, Jeanette.

In her early fifties she, purely by accident, was introduced to a family who needed a godmother for the christening of their son. She obliged and kept in touch with the family for the rest of her life. Sadly, her godson died at quite an early age. Mother continued to do this work while her strength allowed it.

For a very long time my mother had an aversion to travelling; and when asked why, she would respond by saying, "I have travelled half the world and I am weary of travelling." Her travels had not been a holiday. My mother did overcome this aversion in the later stages in her life and she visited several places of pilgrimage, including Lourdes and Fatima. Later, she visited Poland with my father and was reunited with her extended family. This paved the way for us to visit Poland to see for ourselves where our parents were born and to meet our numerous cousins. I have been to Poland on many, many occasions and have very fond memories.

I miss my parents greatly for their good humour, personalities and good counsel. They are irreplaceable and I thank the Creator for their lives.